The Art of
Keeping Good Company

The Art of
Keeping Good Company

LINNETTE RENEE REINDEL

ISBN-13: 9780996204101
ISBN-10: 0996204105
Library of Congress Control Number: 2015904534
Good Company Publishing,
Orlando, FL

Acknowledgments

Dedication

To my mother, *Lorna Reindel*

This book is dedicated to the woman who showed me how to live, how to love, and how to practice the art of keeping good company. Her memory is a daily reminder, that when you give, you also receive.

I'm my best self because of her.

Thank you mom, for teaching me this amazing art form.

Thank you to everyone who sits at my table. I'm grateful to each of you for engaging me, encouraging me, and joining me on the journey that led to this book. You are living proof that I'm keeping good company.

A special thank you to my son, *Adam Wonus*, who arrived at my table as a gift, and earned his seat because of character. *Thank you for embracing and living this art with me.*

Table of Contents

Introduction

$\mathcal{G}$rowing up with an Italian-American mother, the dinner table was the center of our family's universe. But it wasn't because of the food. We didn't have plates piled high with spaghetti and meatballs served to us by a doting mother, forever urging us to "*Mangia! Mangia!*" Rather, our feast was whatever happened to be the catch of the day: potpies, hot dogs, or other inexpensive foods my mother could whip up into something edible for our large family in Toledo, Ohio. (By the way: to this day, I hate potpies!)

My parents were hardworking, blue-collar people (my dad worked in a factory), and they provided us with what they could. Our family had what we needed but not much more. I guess you could say we were poor, but we never realized it. My mother made sure of that. Regardless of what was on our plates, we always looked forward to coming to the table. It was where we went to be together, to reconnect and recharge, to express our thoughts and recount the day's experiences and have them validated by the people we loved. There was always someone eager to weigh in with insights or opinions. Putting your elbows on the table did not signal a lapse in good table manners; it meant you were fully engaged, actively listening and participating in the discussion.

The table was our safe place, and night after night we took our chairs, ready to be nourished by those sitting to our left and right. We never left hungry and we always looked forward to the next meal. This was largely because of the values my mother nurtured in our family. Even though she had only an eleventh-grade education, she was the queen of common sense. "*You are the company you keep*" is something we heard at every meal, because she believed that for better or for worse, the people we chose to hang out with would have an impact on our lives.

At the time, I had no idea how profoundly her words would shape my future. Growing up, there were times when I knew full well I was not keeping good company. Whether it was an untrustworthy friend, an inappropriate boyfriend in high school, or working with the wrong company or coworkers as I got older, I knew deep down that certain relationships were not good for me, but many times I stayed in them because they were familiar or comfortable. I often gave someone a place at my table that they didn't earn or deserve. They took from my table and didn't give anything back, which resulted in my not getting what I needed.

Even worse, they were taking up valuable seating space! They were taking chairs that could have been occupied by people who brought positive things to the table, like opportunities, wisdom, experience, and insights—contributions that would benefit *everyone* at the table.

As I matured, the lesson I learned at my family table— that you are the company you keep—kept coming back to me. I started to watch and wonder: *Why do some people excel in their fields while others fail? Why do some women have rich, nourishing relationships while others feel like outsiders in their own lives? Why do some people act as a magnet for good fortune while others attract what they don't want?*

Gradually, I saw that it's all about creating nourishing, valuable, meaningful relationships, using emotional intelligence to keep those connections vibrant and strong, and excusing those who do not wish to fully participate in those relationships from your table. Successful people know that the company we keep doesn't just happen by chance. We have the power to choose whom we do business with, whom we live with, whom we work for, and whom we invite to join us at our table.

In 2001, I was reminded of this wisdom when a powerful speaker at a professional meeting presented a parable that truly transformed the lesson of keeping good company for me. The speaker was talking about the importance of building a solid, trustworthy team in business—and the message was clear: we are only as good as those who are sitting to our left and right at the proverbial table. The idea is that the people we choose to surround ourselves with can help us or harm us, in large ways and small, in business and in our personal lives. No one can reach all of the good things that are on the table by themselves. We need to be able to *trust* that the people around us will pass those items to us when we want or need them. In turn, we need to be able to reciprocate.

I learned this from my mother first, but I've seen her theory proven in real-life situations again and again.

For me, this lesson of keeping good company has evolved into an art and a way of life. Whenever I am faced with an important decision, I immediately consider who will be sitting on my left and right sides. I ask myself: *"Is this the right company for me? Will this partnership nourish me professionally? Will I grow? Will I have an opportunity to help others grow and become enlightened?"* Not just in business, but also with my family and my personal life, because it all comes down to creating *partnerships.*

Putting this message into practice on a daily basis has not only changed my life, it has defined it. I now view every new situation, every new group of people I work with, and every interview with a prospective employee or employer as a new opportunity to ask myself those important questions. Through this practice, I've learned that anyone—absolutely *everyone*—can benefit from asking these questions and answering them honestly.

Over the years, I have made a commitment to stay connected to this life-changing lesson—*to keep good company*. My mother laid a foundation for me to build upon, life gave me further insights, and each year I gain more clarity from the message. Honoring and living this message has brought me some hard lessons, but ultimately it has taught me to be clear about who I am, what I will tolerate, who will nourish me, and what I'm worth. Most profoundly, it has taught me that not everyone should be invited to join me on my personal or professional journeys. It has taught me that my authentic self is the one who belongs at my table, and that the people to my left and to my right will always play a big part in nourishing that person.

This advice has served me well in my life. I am grateful to know this art and to trust in the magic of it every day. That's why I've shared this message with everyone who sits with me at my table, and why I want to pass it along to you.

One

The Parable

You may have heard this parable while growing up, or maybe it was told to you in a different way. My first experience with it was at a meeting when an inspiring speaker took the podium. Here's the story he told:

There was a woman named Lou, and it was her lucky day—relatively speaking—because on that day she had died. The lucky part: she was immediately greeted by an angel who granted her the choice of where to spend eternity. The angel pulled her close and explained, "Your choice lies behind either door number one or door number two, and you get to choose. Are you ready?"

Realizing that her choice was important, Lou asked if she could look behind each door before selecting. The angel replied, "Of course! This is your lucky day! Let's take a look."

As the angel guided Lou to door number one, Lou noticed the door was massive, with intricate carvings no doubt laid by the most gifted of craftsmen. A solid brass handle gave the enormous, thick door an impressive texture and an aura of prestige. As the door was opened and Lou took her first step inside, she couldn't help but be drawn into this powerful room, which held a table that appeared to go on forever—a table with a top made of thick, dark, heavy wood supported by massive legs made from the same solid, rich wood, set with more food than she had ever seen. The table held an endless variety of dishes: meats, vegetables, baskets of fruits, platters of the finest cheeses and breads, a feast fit for any king or queen. Lou was certain the feast before her eyes was meant to nourish all who encountered this table.

Upon stepping further into the room, she noticed all the people around the table. There was a person in every chair. The chairs themselves were strong and beautiful, and as she drew closer, she realized that every person at the table had a fork and spoon handcuffed to their wrists. However, each fork and spoon was much longer than normal, making it impossible for the people to feed themselves. When she realized that everyone at the table was thin and pale with sunken eyes—and looked malnourished—she stepped back in shock. Angry and frustrated by their inability to feed themselves, many of the people had become disengaged from the table out of sheer exhaustion.

Horrified, Lou anxiously turned to the angel and said, "May I look behind door number two?"

"Of course," responded the angel.

At door number two, Lou noticed that the door had the same impressively massive appearance and solid brass handle as the first. And when the door opened, she found the table and chairs to be the same and there was a similar abundance of food, with many choices, textures, colors, and amazing aromas that captured her senses. Stepping further into the room, she noticed that every chair around the table was filled, and here, too, the people had very long forks and spoons handcuffed to their wrists. As Lou leaned in more closely, she was taken aback by the stark difference between this table and the previous one. Every person sitting at this table was laughing, animated, and engaged in the feast. They were all well nourished and thriving as they enjoyed the abundance of what was in front of them.

Lou felt confused. She turned to the angel and said, "I don't understand. Everything was exactly the same behind each door: the table and chairs, more food than any one person could ever desire, and everyone at each table had the same oversize fork and spoon handcuffed to their wrists. How can those behind the first door be so weak, malnourished, angry, and literally falling off their chairs, while those behind the second door are well nourished, thriving, and fully enjoying the experience and the abundance before them?"

The angel took Lou's hand and said, "Life is about choices and options. You see, those who chose door number two understood they could not feed themselves with the oversize fork and spoon, but they also realized that by looking to their left and right they could feed those next to them, and in return they would be fed. They are aware of who they are, what they need, and who is sitting at their table. They have learned to invite good company—those who will look out for one another's well-being, people they can trust.

"They also live by and embrace these principles," the angel continued. "They have grown and adapted to be able to fully utilize their larger-than-life forks and spoons. They understand and accept that what seemed impossible to reach is actually available to them thanks to the help and goodwill of the company they are keeping. They understand that if this consistent rhythm of giving and receiving is interrupted by even one person at the table, then they all risk not being able to enjoy or benefit from the feast before them. As a result, they also know not to be afraid to remove a chair or push one back from the table when necessary. They live the most important lesson—that of keeping good company."

The angel had shared a profound truth with Lou, who said simply, "I understand. I have made my choice." And with that, she stepped through door number two.

Two

The Table

Until I heard the parable, I thought I knew what I wanted and needed, both personally and professionally. And I thought I had mastered the art of keeping good company, as my mother had taught me. But honestly, things didn't feel quite right in my life. Although I was surrounded by lots of friends and a big family, I was merely surviving and not thriving. Sometimes I was doing things just to do them; I wasn't participating to my fullest potential or stretching myself to go beyond my comfort zone. In my career, I was not moving forward in a productive way that would allow me to feel truly fulfilled or as though I was serving a worthwhile purpose by empowering others. Nor was I holding other people or myself accountable for developing richer, deeper relationships.

Something was missing from my approach to life. Hearing the parable caused me to pause and consider my choices up until that point. What did the people behind door number two have that I didn't? *Clarity!* Every person at that table knew what they wanted. They knew how to reach for and ask for what was in front of them—a miraculous act that happens only when you know who you are and what you need and have the courage to seek it.

In real life, the challenge is that if you don't have a realistic pulse on what inspires you, what makes you unique, and what your wants and needs are, it's hard to feel fulfilled and it's difficult to lead an authentic life. But the answers can only come from you, so it's worth asking some very important questions: *Who am I? What do I want for myself? What do I want from others?* If you don't know what you want, you're not going to get it. There is a saying that goes, "You teach people how you want to be treated." Hearing the parable made me pay attention to this truism and ultimately change my life for the better, and I believe it can do the same for anyone who chooses to take it to heart.

After hearing the story of Lou and the angel, I realized that I create my own table, that I don't have to sit with people in my life just because they're there. I don't have to participate with them. I have choices. There should be a give-and-take in relationships, and if there isn't, it's okay to push certain chairs back from the table and make space for new participants. I also realized that I needed to start giving myself permission to act on these choices and desires regardless of what the outcome might be, or I would risk missing out on life's abundance of opportunities.

In thinking about who I am, deep down inside, and what I wanted and needed, the image of the thriving table behind door number two stayed with me. At first I considered the scene as a whole—the large table with an abundance of food, an amazing feast being shared by many people, each extending their forks and spoons to one another in continuous harmony and rhythm. I realized that what really made this table more desirable than the other one was the people sitting around it. They were fully participating and extending their utensils for the good of those around them; they were creating a give-and-get rhythm. They had figured out how to help one another and, in turn, help themselves.

Then I started thinking about the individual elements in each scene and the meaning behind each one. I decided to start with the table, because the table represents your identity—your foundation, your core beliefs and values, and how you choose to *live* them every day. Really, in essence, it's your authentic self, who you are deep down when it's just you, when no one else is watching. You might wonder: Why is knowing yourself really so important, so life affirming or life changing? I think it's because when you present your genuine self to the world, when you clearly communicate who you are and you live authentically, you will attract the people you want and need to your table.

To gain clarity about what makes your "table"—your core identity and values—unique, think, for a moment, about your last job interview. You probably arrived looking polished in your best suit or dress, ready to offer your prospective employer a glossy overview of your past successes and how you would best contribute to the team. You were prepared to tell the interviewer about your strengths and how you've overcome your weaknesses. When the inevitable request, "Tell me about yourself" came, you were primed to respond with all that you had—a fabulous list of adjectives that sum you up. It was probably your best-pitch effort to win over the interviewer.

But wait—pause for a moment and really think about this. How did you describe yourself in unique terms? What words did you choose? Did you describe yourself as *loyal, trustworthy, responsible, a problem solver*? As *innovative, prompt, patient*, or *diplomatic*? Did you share that you were a self-starter or a compassionate leader? Now, put yourself in the prospective employer's shoes—do those words really mean anything? Do they give a clear image of the person you're interviewing? Do they provide a sense of context? No, they don't. Like an impressionist painting, these words merely give a general idea of the person's form, but all the important details—the ones that really distinguish one person from the next—are fuzzy.

In my case, I knew I was kind and loyal and courageous, lived with integrity, possessed solid leadership skills, and was supportive and entrepreneurial. I had all the attributes someone would look for in a trusted family member, a good friend, and certainly a valued employee, but intuitively I knew there was more to me than that. After hearing the parable, it dawned on me that I was falling short, that I never really shared the true essence of myself. I knew I was bigger than the words I commonly used to describe myself. I knew I was more than *kind*, *courageous*, and *loyal*. But I didn't know how to access the deeper aspects of myself or how to articulate them until I heard the parable.

That's when it hit me. Instead of using abstract adjectives, I decided to describe myself as a table—that's right: a table, my table. By doing that, suddenly there was something more tangible, more concrete and engaging, and I found my word choices to be organic and free flowing. This was the moment when I fully understood the value of self-clarity and discovered how to share who I am in the most powerful way. I realized how beneficial it is to do this on many levels. Not only does it convey self-understanding, self-awareness, and a willingness to share your authentic self, but it also shows that you've taken the time to really think about what's important and who you are, to dig deeper and get to the meaningful stuff, which helps draw more interesting and genuine people your way.

This is how I chose to describe myself: My table is traditional in design with a top that's well crafted from solid pine, which is typically a soft wood, but this one is a thick, rich cut, and it's supported by unbreakable wrought-iron legs. The oblong shape stretches with great vastness and embraces the uniqueness of the surrounding chairs, which are made of solid wood and have seats with textured fabrics. The top of my table is not smooth—rather, it is filled with unique knots and nicks that are either part of the wood itself or left over from the friends I have invited to my table—markings that give my table uncommon character.

When I first described myself in this way, I got reactions I had never received before. People sat up and paid attention to the image I used to describe my most authentic self—my core self. Like the wood on my tabletop, I appear to be gentle and soft (particularly my voice), but I am a strong and capable person. My courage and faith serve me well thanks to the many lessons I've learned, and I'm not afraid to share them. I think about things and question them on a deep level; the surface alone doesn't interest me. More importantly, by describing myself in this way, I allowed people to connect to the truest parts of me—the parts that are strong and resilient and have an unbreakable foundation, and the open and welcoming parts, too. It allows people to see me as someone who strives daily for integrity, yet embraces her imperfections.

I decided to try this exercise with other people. One Friday night my sister, my sister-in-law, my niece, and I were sitting together and I was sharing how describing yourself as a table could be a very enlightening and powerful self-discovery tool. I asked each of them to describe themselves in this fashion. My sister-in-law Beth volunteered first. Before I tell you what she said, let me tell you who I thought she was: I met Beth for the first time when she was thirteen. She has been married to my brother for more than twenty-five years. She is a beautiful woman, one who is frequently mistaken for the actress Sandra Bullock, and she is a brilliant interior designer, yet she lacks confidence in her abilities, both personally and professionally. Beth is a very private person, not someone you'd immediately consider warm and friendly or highly expressive. In all the years I've known her, I have seen her cry only twice. Some people might describe her cool demeanor as being stuck-up or antisocial because she rarely shares her concerns or fears with others; however, there is something besides her Hollywood beauty that draws you in.

Very deliberately, Beth placed her hands on the table, leaned in, and shared the following: "My table is small; it's always set for no more than four. However, it expands when I need it to. With its many layers, it extends with great length and can provide seats for many people, and I actually quite like it when it is open."

In that moment I felt like I had met the authentic Beth for the first time: a woman who appears reserved and holds back her emotions, who opens up when the need or desire arises, has tremendous depth, and truly appreciates those around her. Being able to expose her core self in a non-threatening way, and her desire to find ways to remain open more often, helped Beth share that she's not the way people perceive her to be. Through the table metaphor she communicated to us that even though she's accustomed to a table for two or four, she's ready to invite more guests to her table and engage fully with them. *I had no idea!*

Discovering this about Beth helped me better understand and appreciate her perspective. Yes, she's cool and reserved on the outside, but she's warm and inviting within. And our relationship has gradually become richer and closer because she has allowed herself to open up and reveal her true self with me. Ever since that relationship-changing conversation took place, we have enjoyed each other's company more. Professionally, Beth is doing better as a designer than she ever has, and I think it's because she's more willing to open up and let others appreciate her on an intimate level.

Personally, when I discovered what my own table looked like—the core of who I was—I made the choice to live in accord with my true self. That's when certain feelings became crystal clear: I recognized that I like my uniqueness, including my strengths and imperfections. I wanted more from my life personally and professionally, and I did not feel like I should have to apologize for that. Suddenly, I knew that all the unfulfilling relationships and lack of momentum in my career in the past were brought on by my own lack of clarity.

Thanks to these insights, I started holding myself more accountable for my life. And I made a choice to improve it by keeping in mind what my table looks like and letting it guide my decisions. Once I made that change, my world opened in ways I could have never imagined. New opportunities for personal and professional growth, nourishment, and fulfillment flowed into my life, all because I had made a choice to know and honor myself.

In this book, my goal is to show you how you, too, can keep good company in every aspect of your life. I am confident that by learning to live this art you will develop peace of mind, a better rhythm to your life, and greater confidence through knowing yourself deep down. You'll also realize that when you're clear about who you are and what you want and when you're with the right people, there are an abundance of appealing opportunities right in front of you. It's up to you to take them. They're there. They're yours. All you have to do is extend yourself and ask for what you want.

So take the first step toward setting your table. Describe yourself using a table metaphor. *What does your table look like?* Reflect on the image that comes to mind, describe it, and feel the power of the adjectives you choose. Then, consider: *Are you living in accord with this image? If not, are you ready to start? And what would it take for you to do that?* Next, share this image with trusted friends or family members, people who really know and understand you. Pay attention to how they react and think about what their responses suggest about whether or not you're living in sync with your core values.

Three

The Chairs

*I*f you've ever thrown a dinner party, you know that the guest list can make or break the spirit of the event. The same thing was true in the parable. After all, the sturdy, endless table and the bountiful feast were similar behind door number one and door number two; the element that distinguished one scene from the other was not the chairs, but the people occupying them.

Remember that upon closer inspection behind door number one, Lou noticed the people looked sad, depressed, and angry. They were not engaging or interacting with one another, and they were unable to feed themselves with the unusually long forks and spoons handcuffed to their wrists. By contrast, the people behind door number two were engaged, happy, thriving, vibrant, and completely aware of the people to their left and right. Their ability to look in each direction provided access to the abundance before them. While they realized it was impossible to get their own forks and spoons to their mouths, they recognized that by simply turning to their left and right and extending their utensils to those next to them, they could feed one another. So why couldn't table number one be more like table number two?

The difference reflected who was in the chairs. The people at table number two actively chose to engage one another and participate in the feast because they knew what they wanted and needed and what they could offer others. They were thoughtful and astute enough to know how to give to others and how to ask for help getting what they needed. They weren't motivated to push others aside and feed themselves at other people's expense. They had a keen sense of reciprocity. Basically, they were willing to sit at the table and share, and they knew that at the end of the day, there was plenty to go around. What's more, they chose to surround themselves with others who were equally self-aware and self-empowered.

N ow take a look at your own table and feel its inherent power. As you begin to recognize and live in accordance with your essential values, you will quickly understand that you are accountable for everything that happens to you "at your table." It's your responsibility to choose whom you invite or disinvite. As the keeper of your table, you have the power to add chairs and move chairs closer to or farther from your table. You also have the power to excuse those who are incapable of extending themselves in a positive way. For example, when there is someone in your life who takes and takes and doesn't give in return, leaving you feeling empty and unsatisfied—that's a person who may not respect you or your table. You need to give yourself permission to ask that person to move away from your table for a while, or to excuse him or her from the table entirely.

It's important to note that I never felt there was a particular number of people or chairs that had to be at my table. The key was to experience the right rhythm, a spirit of give-and-take and active participation from those present at my table.

Now take a closer look at the chairs surrounding your table. Undoubtedly, there are empty chairs at your table, perhaps one, two, five, or more; the number is not important. The question is: Are you feeling the urge to fill them with people you already know and are acquainted with? Are you longing to be surrounded by family members, old friends, past and present coworkers, or those from your spouse's, partner's, and/or children's circles? It is time to evaluate those who are sitting in chairs around your table and to become comfortable with the empty chairs that remain. Do not fill them to just fill them. Remember that the number of chairs or people at your table does not determine your worth.

So before you reflexively invite the usual suspects to your table, pause and be deliberate and thoughtful about whom you choose to invite. Select those who will willingly and passionately bring their unique points of view, ideas, and life experiences to your table. Choose people who can provide you with a sense of grounding and unconditional, nonjudgmental support. You'll also want to include individuals who will add a new perspective, enrich your knowledge base, enlighten you, provide you with networking or growth opportunities, and bring depth into your conversations. All of these qualities will provide richness to the experience of sitting at your table. This is really about identifying who's good for you, who supports you, and who adds richness to your life—and who doesn't. To some extent, you'll have to trust your instincts about whether someone is a good source of company for you or whether being with him or her feels right to you (based on your mood, energy level, and other subtle signals when you're with that person). It's important to embrace the art of adjustment and be willing to change the guest list and the seating arrangement at your table as your needs and circumstances shift.

In my own life, I tend to see potential guests in three categories, and I like to think of them as occupying certain types of chairs, with varying degrees of permanence:

- There are those I *know* I want at my table—they get an automatic invitation. For me, that might be a strong, reliable friend that I think of as occupying a solid, wooden, Shaker-style chair, or an interesting colleague who has fresh, creative insights and sits in a funky but sturdy acrylic chair, or a nurturing, comforting, dependable family member who resides in a soothing rocking chair. Right now, my grown son sits in a big, leather office chair at my table because he is all business as he builds his career.

- There are those whose company I feel obligated to keep, even if I don't always enjoy or benefit from it. These people might use a folding chair that can be removed from the table, as needed, folded up and put in a corner until they are ready to be fully engaged or actively participate. These people may not be on the permanent guest list; I can change my mind as my needs change or as their behavior and level of engagement changes.

- Then, there are those I'm not entirely sure about, and the structure of their chairs often reflects my uncertain feelings. These folks might occupy lawn chairs, if they're easygoing and flexible but not always engaged. My brother, for example, tends to check in and out, so I think of him as sitting in a lawn chair. When he's available, we engage in a meaningful way, and it is always an easy, relaxing experience, like sitting together in a tranquil park, but we don't connect that often. Alternatively, the people in this category might occupy a stool if they have a tendency to belly up to the table when it suits them, then disengage when it doesn't. Or they may sit in a chair with wheels if they often come in and out of focus and vary in their level of participation.

If you look at people this way, you'll be more realistic about what you can expect from them, and you'll be less likely to be disappointed when you don't get more from them. But remember that over time, people can shift from one category to another or one type of chair to another—and that's okay. The types of chairs you allow at your table are also flexible. At any given time or stage of your life, the key is to consider who will help you and your table thrive.

To be honest, I love that I have so many different chairs and people at my table. In fact, I quickly learned that I have multiple tables, each representing a different aspect of my life. You may have several tables as well—for example, a "work table," a "family table," a "friends table," and so on.

Throughout life, and throughout any given day, we will move from one table to another, but the same principles apply at each one. I realize that as long as I remain clear about the company I choose to keep at each table and fully understand what I can expect from them, I know whom to sit with, and where, and when.

The act of embracing my tables in this way has proven to be so empowering, not only for me but for those who are seated around me as well. Let me explain what I mean by this. For a long time, at my chosen "family table," there was just my only sister, the best sister I could ask for—always supportive (even at 1:00 a.m. when I could not sleep) and kind, and always my steadfast cheerleader. She's younger than I am, but there have been many times when she has been wiser and kept me in check about my own behavior. Often I would seek her counsel when I wanted to discuss something very important to me, something that was potentially life changing, like whether to move or be with a particular boyfriend. But rather than coming away from the discussion feeling empowered and enlightened, I often felt frustrated, as though I wasn't being truly heard or nourished from our discussions.

Before I discovered what I needed at my table, these feelings of frustration and yearning for more would occur after most of our conversations. Then, one day when I was talking to her about whether to change jobs and move across the country, I realized that she had no frame of reference from which to guide me. She simply couldn't give me the insight or perspective I needed during those conversations. It didn't mean she didn't want to; she just didn't have the experiences to draw from or the knowledge to nourish me or provide the insight I needed right then. Rather than assume she didn't care about me and rather than excuse her from my life, I realized that what I was seeking was probably best found at my "friends table." I was looking to the wrong left and right, and I needed to have more realistic expectations of the people I was inviting to each of my tables or whom I was depending on. It's important to remember that if people aren't equipped to give you what you need from them, it's not their fault, and it doesn't mean there isn't value in having them be a part of your life; you need to be clear about whether your expectations are being applied to the right people.

Once I realized the importance of looking to my right and left in the appropriate settings, it became easier to have my needs fulfilled, without drama or disappointment. I gained clarity about whom to have which conversations with and what I could reasonably expect from different people. My sister was not someone I could count on to nourish me in the way I needed when it came to making major professional or relationship decisions. But I accept and love my sister for who she is. And I still wanted her at my family table because I treasure all the other ways she feeds me— namely, by offering unconditional sisterly love and support. This realization greatly benefited our relationship because she had felt like she was disappointing me; once we removed this unnecessary pressure from our relationship, it began to thrive again.

⁓

Now that you understand the value of the chair space, it's time to look around your own table. Enjoy those who are fully engaged and take note of which chairs need to be vacated, moved, or pushed back—in other words, who will be invited or disinvited. Most of all, embrace the possibility of who will join you and what they can bring to the table. As long as everyone is participating, whether it's by providing unconditional love and support (like my sister), expertise or advice on a specific topic (like a valued colleague), a new adventure or experience (like an outgoing friend), or bits of wisdom or perspective (which can come from almost anyone you trust), there is a place for them at one of your tables.

When it comes to hosting your table, don't sit and wait for the right dynamic to happen naturally. Create it! Give yourself the courage to make these choices, to be clear about your needs and which people can fulfill them. It's okay for the chairs to be different and for there to be movement to and from the table. Life is a shifting work in progress; your table can be, too. As long as your table feels right to you at any given time in your life, it is right. That's how you'll master the art of keeping good company.

Four

The Fork and Spoon

ithout the right utensils, it's difficult to nourish yourself or anyone else in your life. In the parable, by looking at the two tables, it was clear that survival depends on being able to feed yourself (or not); it was also clear that we thrive when we feed others because we can receive as we give. That's a truism for real life. Not only is giving its own reward because it nourishes us from the inside out, but giving freely to others increases the likelihood that they'll reciprocate, and that everyone's needs will be met in the end.

In my life, I have encountered many people who have impressive talents and skills and the potential to do great things in the world. And yet, I'm constantly surprised by how many people feel that what they want and need in order to achieve their personal greatness is totally out of reach and just not "realistic" for them. Maybe this feeling strikes a chord with you.

Have you ever been told that you couldn't achieve something because you lacked the resources, or that it was for someone more educated, prettier, stronger, or taller? That what you wanted was unacceptable or unrealistic? That you didn't deserve it? Or maybe you felt like those incredible opportunities just weren't available for someone like you. To some extent, these feelings may stem from keeping the wrong company—from spending too much time with negative people who hold you back or chip away at your confidence—but it can also come from inside you.

The truth is, a variety of appealing experiences and opportunities are right in front of you, whether you recognize them or not. And you don't have to wait to pursue them—if you have the abilities and skills, you can begin reaching for them now; if you don't, it's time to begin cultivating the tools that will allow you to explore and receive what you truly desire in life.

In the parable, door number two opened to an appealing table, an abundance of food, thoughtful and generous people who happened to have longer than normal forks and spoons. But they knew how to use those tools to help others and thus help themselves. As the parable clearly unveils, there is no secret to having and experiencing what you truly desire. First, you have to see the tools you've been given for what they are, then you have to discover or rediscover how to properly use them.

The people at table number one chose not to learn how to use those tools to their advantage. As a result, they allowed themselves to slouch away from the table, overcome by frustration and malnourishment. Those sitting around the second table quickly discovered that by extending their utensils to their neighbors, they could feed and be fed. They recognized that being able to put their utensils to good use meant the difference between thriving, growing, and enjoying themselves—or not.

Discovering the symbolic meaning of the fork and the spoon in the parable had a powerful impact on me. That's the essence of what I'm sharing with you in this book and what I hope will stay with you long after you put it down. I started thinking about my own "utensils for life"—the tools that have the power to feed and nourish me as well as those I care about. We are each taught very early on how to use a fork and a spoon; it's a learned skill and a gift, one that grows and attaches itself to us so we are never without these skills.

I remember when my son Adam was little, learning how to use his utensils, his tiny new "fork and spoon" (a.k.a., a "spork"). Most of the time what was on that little fork and spoon never made it to his mouth. With every miss, he would look to me for help and each time, I would offer my assistance to ensure that he was nourished and received what he desired. Gradually, over time, he mastered the art of feeding himself.

As he grew, he realized that the fork and spoon he had grown accustomed to using were no longer doing what they had done in the past; no longer could he always have what was right in front of him. When he looked to me for help, as he did before, he did not always get what he wanted because it was no longer just about food; it had become about how to seize opportunities, adventures, and new experiences in his life, ones that would help him grow.

The opportunities were abundant, and being the child that he was, he wanted them all. For me, as an active member of his table, the delicate balance was to live and model the art of giving and receiving. Of course, I wanted to give to him, and most times I felt it was my responsibility. (After all, who else was going to give him what he needed and wanted, if not the mother who loved him with all her heart?) As he grew up, however, the times I gave so freely decreased. I wanted him to master how to use his much larger fork and spoon and to better understand the importance of looking to his left and right, not just to me.

Often, my son felt it was unfair of me to refuse to extend my utensils to him without any reciprocity. He would sit at the proverbial table, feeling angry, experiencing a sense of entitlement. The reality was by then, Adam had been given a much larger fork and spoon. They had grown as he had and it was time for him to learn how to use them, to see what they were capable of gathering—new insights, opportunities, and resources—for him.

By the time his college graduation was approaching, we had several conversations about his immediate future—what he would do, where he would work, where he would live. Adam was convinced that he would just come home for a few months to catch his breath and determine what he wanted. I had always told him that I would provide whatever he required through his college years and that when college ended, he should be prepared to provide for himself. I gave him plenty of notice—eighteen years! I encouraged him to pay attention to that notice, to be prepared for that change, and I told him that moving back home was not going to be an option.

Please understand it wasn't that I didn't want him back home. I did! But knowing what I knew and having lived this art of giving and receiving, I did not want to provide a disservice to the most important person at my table. I had to push his chair back from my table for a period of time—for his own good. Adam needed to learn how to extend his fork and spoon to me and to others around the table he created for himself. If I hadn't pushed Adam's chair away from my table, I wouldn't have helped him to thrive on his own. He would have lived in my debt with no sense of responsibility or his own abilities or potential but with a sense of entitlement, a belief that I would and should continue to be his provider. Adam had the tools; all he had to do was look around and figure out how to use them, which is ultimately what he did.

A few days after graduation, Adam decided to join a friend who was moving to Orlando, Florida, to search for work. Adam applied for many jobs, expanded his table by exploring various interests and meeting new people, and began to partake of the astonishing feast that was placed in front of him. He started networking and asking questions. He began to probe deeper about what he thought he wanted while staying open to other possibilities. He asked for help and guidance from other people, and he invited people who had different perspectives, who were more experienced or more educated, who were well versed and clear about what they wanted for themselves, to sit at his table. He became comfortable with rearranging his table without fear of loss but with the hope of more gain.

This is difficult for many people to do; they often hold on to relationships or jobs years after they should have left, simply because they're afraid of moving out of their comfort zone or they expect someone else to fix what's missing in their lives. They're unwilling to adjust the seating arrangement at their own tables. Adam quickly realized that his current circumstances and company were unlikely to get him to the next stage of his life, so he opened the chairs at his table to new people.

All the forks and spoons that began to feed Adam came his way because he embraced the art and rhythm of giving and receiving, of feeding and being fed. He gained clarity about what he wanted and what was next for him, and he began to practice the art of keeping good company by inviting people who could help him move to the next level of his life. If he wanted a job or to travel or to gain greater life experiences, he knew it was not his mother's responsibility—or anyone else's—to provide that for him; he had to find a way to cultivate those opportunities for himself by visiting many different tables, engaging with others, giving of himself, and asking for help in return. Time and time again, I shared with Adam this simple message: *If you give, you will get.* Gradually, he realized that by extending his fork and spoon to feed others, he made it possible for more opportunities to flow into his life and into the lives of everyone at his table.

Although it wasn't an easy transition, this time for Adam was life changing. He not only learned how to set a bountiful table for himself, one that offers amazing possibilities for growth; he also learned how to be a more active participant at other people's tables, including mine. For the first time in more than twenty years, I could call upon him for support or guidance or just a stimulating conversation—without feeling like he wanted something from me as his mother. This was when I began to think of him as a truly active participant at my table, rather than simply someone I wanted to have there because I love him.

I'll give you an example. After Adam graduated from college I was involved in a not-so-good relationship. Adam would call or come to visit and share his thoughts and ideas, not as a child but as a man. One day he said to me, "You deserve all of life's best and I expect you to know this and live as you have taught me." It was a powerful dose of my own advice, and something I needed to hear. Essentially, he reminded me that if you want more from other people, you have to ask for it and you have to know your worth. Adam began holding me accountable to the lessons I had taught him. In a sense, he turned the table on me in the best possible way! To this day, I know that when I need support or someone to listen or provide me with a different perspective that's brutally honest, Adam is at my table, ready to be a wise and active participant who will gladly offer me his spoon and fork.

A s Adam discovered, getting what you want in life can only happen when you have learned to use the tools you've been given. Many people spend their entire lives struggling to get their own fork and spoon to their mouth; few realize that if they simply extended themselves to help those who are next to them, their own wants and needs could be attained much more easily.

That's why it's important for all of us to learn and relearn how to properly use our utensils, to master the art of reaching toward others and embracing a spirit of give-and-take in our lives. Once you appreciate the tools you have and figure out how to use them optimally, you'll set a table for yourself that will allow you to grow and thrive in all sorts of ways you didn't expect. That's when the art of flourishing really happens.

Five

The Feast

*I*n the parable, there was plenty of food to go around and there was no end to the feast. To me, the sheer abundance, the varied choices, and the seemingly endless possibilities symbolized the many opportunities and experiences that were right in front of me in my own life—travel, education, adventure, meeting new people, spiritual enlightenment, and more. The "feast" represented desires and opportunities I hadn't realized were available to me.

Until I began to live by the art of keeping good company, I thought the notion of having it all was about money, power, and good luck. *I was so wrong!* It's about inviting the right people to my table, people who know how to use their utensils effectively, people I can learn from. It's about surrounding myself with people who stimulate me professionally, personally, and spiritually, and having people in my life that I can engage in meaningful, powerful, and literally life-changing conversations. Most of all, it's about being clear with myself about what I want and asking the right questions of those around me, while being open to constructive feedback. It's about fully extending myself to others to keep that constant, fulfilling rhythm flowing. Is it really that simple? *Yes!*

For many years now, I have been in a relationship with the most amazing man who happens to climb mountains. I have no interest in climbing a hill, let alone a mountain, but every weekend he'd ask me to go for "a short hike." These hikes are not short, and they always include hills (big hills!). One day, a few years ago, I agreed; it was my way of extending myself to him. I gave myself a pep talk that I could do it and I was determined to show him that I could get to the top. About halfway up this so-called hill, I started crying. I was hot and I couldn't breathe, so we stopped, sat down, and I cried some more. I told him that I thought he was setting me up to fail, that he knew it would be hard for me and that I did not think I could get to the top. He sat down with me on the ground and told me he would never set me up to fail. After a long pause, he said the most profound thing: "I didn't bring you or ask you to join me with the goal of reaching the top. I brought you with me so you could enjoy the journey."

He asked me to look around and take in the beauty that was right in front of me. He told me that most climbers do not count on getting to the top; to them, success is counted in the number of incredible journeys they experience. He went on to say that if I approached my work as a journey and wasn't so focused on reaching the top, I would have already arrived and I would be enjoying the view and my life more. Here was someone at my table who handed me the most incredible spoonful of advice, wisdom, and opportunity, and he did it with such love and admiration for me that it took my breath away. His was a lesson I truly took to heart!

These days, more than ever, I am fully committed and passionate about sitting with the right people, looking to my left and right at all times, and never missing the extension of someone else's fork or spoon. My feast is set with great jobs, amazing travel experiences, being a single mother to a child who has grown into a brilliant man, being a good source of support to my family and friends, having the opportunity to write this book and engage others as a public speaker, and more. These experiences have allowed me to fulfill my life's purpose as a brave, self-actualized, confident, graceful woman. All of this (and so much more) would have been lost or left unrealized if I had not learned the art of keeping good company, if I hadn't been influenced, inspired, and assisted by those I have invited to my tables.

Meanwhile, I try to stay open to the endless possibilities that continue to be laid out before me. I want to keep filling myself with life's abundant feast of experiences and challenges and master the art of giving to others with grace. In my mind, there's no end to the feast; it keeps going and going throughout life.

Six

The Invitations

S urely you've heard the saying that one weak link can break the chain. Well, the same thing is true when one person doesn't fully participate at the table. Consider it your responsibility to ensure that this never happens at *your* table—no weak links allowed! Pay attention to what is happening to your left and to your right at each of your tables, so that you will feel nourished by the company you choose to keep and you can set yourself and others up to thrive.

Before you put this book down, I encourage you to pause for a moment and picture your own options. Imagine that you're standing in front of two doors that offer different choices of how, where, and with whom you will keep company. Behind door number one, there's a place to sit at a table with familiar faces. You will be fed minimally, enough to survive, but you'll continue to feel hungry, empty, or frustrated most of the time. Behind door number two, there's also a chair for you, but this one is at a table with an abundance of options and people who have a zest for life (some who you know, and others you don't), people who will clearly support your needs and reciprocate when you give to them. This setting will provide the opportunity for you to thrive and be filled and fulfilled in so many ways.

So which one will you choose?

Perhaps your answer has shifted after reading this book, as mine did when I first heard the parable. Think back to when you first described yourself using the table metaphor, selecting words to describe the essence of who you are in the most authentic way possible, maybe for the very first time in your life. (If you haven't already shared that experience with someone you're close to, I encourage you to do it soon!) Think about when you really looked around your table and thought about who should be excused, who should be moved, and who is missing from your table. Don't be afraid to leave some chairs empty for now; save them for new people you meet, people who will truly nourish you and who will graciously accept your nourishment in return.

Now that you've given this idea some careful reflection, allow yourself to devise your own rules for table manners, then choose and create a table that reflects your current wants and needs, your desires and dreams. Invite the people you value and respect most in your life. Designing your table in this fashion will set you on a journey of abundance, fulfillment, and unlimited possibilities. Once you've created the table you want, go ahead and put your elbows on it, lean in and become engaged with the marvelous individuals sitting to your left and right.

You are ready to truly live the art of keeping good company. Relish the pleasure of their companionship and influence—and enjoy the feast you create for one another!

Final Thoughts:

Table Manners

*A*s I started to invite people to join me at the various tables I was consciously creating in my life, I started thinking about the table manners with which I was raised. We all carry some of the same rules from our childhood into adulthood, but I realized that we don't necessarily have to follow them at our own present-day tables. It didn't take long for me to realize that just as I had created my own table(s), I could create my own table manners. After all, these are my tables, and the manners I choose to follow will govern my new behavior and the behavior of everyone at these tables.

Taking stock of the table manners that had been instilled in me, I began questioning which ones made sense and which ones really didn't. I decided I wanted to change things in an enlightened way, based on what I view as respectful or disrespectful, courteous or discourteous, today. Now that I have my own tables, the rules are up to me, and I can inject my own ideas of how people can best interact, open up, and thrive. With that goal in mind, I decided to rewrite the rules.

Here is a list of the ten table manners my own mother or my friends' mothers taught me, followed by the revamped versions I choose to abide by these days.

"SIT UP STRAIGHT."

Get comfortable and enjoy what's around you. The table doesn't have to be so formal; get what you need and be yourself.

"DON'T PUT YOUR ELBOWS ON THE TABLE."

Put your elbows on the table and lean in, because that means you're engaged, involved, and fully participating in the conversation.

"PLACE YOUR NAPKIN ON YOUR LAP."

Put your napkin where you can reach it, so you know it's there when you need it. It's there to be used; trust yourself to decide what that means.

"DON'T TALK WITH YOUR MOUTH FULL."

Talk until you're full of good conversation, direction, clarity, a sense of personal connection, or whatever you're seeking from the table—and you feel fulfilled.

"THANK THE HOST."

Be thankful that you're in good company and be grateful to yourself for choosing to consciously surround yourself with good company.

"USE YOUR PROPER UTENSILS."

You only need a fork and spoon, one utensil for each hand so you can pass along information to your left and right and receive from both directions as well.

"NO SINGING AT THE TABLE."

Sing to your heart's content. Express what you feel, think, and wish—until you feel satisfied.

"ASK TO BE EXCUSED."

Excuse others from the table as necessary; take full control of your table and disinvite those who don't deserve a place setting.

"EAT EVERYTHING ON YOUR PLATE."

Sample everything at least once. You might as well try everything because if you don't, you'll never know if you like something new. You'll only be cheating yourself.

"SAY PLEASE AND THANK YOU."

Say please and thank you. My mother was right about this one. Using these words reflects good manners, the essence of being respectful and polite. It's still important and timeless at any table!

⌣⟶

Remember that the manners you have carried over from your family of origin may or may not apply to your table today. Because you have set your own table, you can determine which manners and guidelines are permissible there. Think about what makes sense for who and how you are today. As I have, you may want to keep some of the table manners you were raised with, while revising or discarding others. It's up to you to set the tone and the style and to determine what's okay and what's not. It's your life, so you get to rewrite your table manners. But keep this in mind: as my mother taught me, we teach people how we want to be treated, so it's important to establish parameters, expectations, and manners that work for you now.

22706317R00041

Made in the USA
San Bernardino, CA
17 July 2015